JACOBY 2NT

PRACTICE YOUR BIDDING

Master Point Press
331 Douglas Avenue
Toronto, Ontario, Canada
M5M 1H2

(416) 781-0351   Internet: **www.masterpointpress.com**

National Library of Canada Cataloguing in Publication

Seagram, Barbara
        Jacoby 2NT / Barbara Seagram & Linda Lee.

(Practice your bidding)
ISBN 1-894154-61-4

1. Contract bridge--Bidding. I. Lee, Linda (Linda Marcia), 1947- II. Title. III. Series.

GV1282.4.S4195 2003   795.41'52   C2003-902592-6

Design and layout: Olena S. Sullivan/New Mediatrix
Editor: Ray Lee

Printed and bound in Canada by Webcom Limited

1 2 3 4 5 6 7   09 08 07 06 05 04 03

JACOBY 2NT

Barbara Seagram & Linda Lee

MASTER POINT PRESS • TORONTO

The
PRACTICE YOUR BIDDING
Series

Jacoby 2NT

Roman Keycard Blackwood

Splinter Bids

Practice Your Slam Bidding (CD-ROM)

TABLE OF CONTENTS

HOW TO USE THIS BOOK

The purpose of this book is to help you and your partner practice the Jacoby 2NT convention and understand better how it is used. The book has been designed so it can be used either on your own or working with a partner. But while you will certainly get a lot out of it if you use it alone, it is especially good to use this book with your favourite partner to make sure that you are both on the same wavelength.

The first section of the book provides a refresher for the Jacoby 2NT convention. It has lots of examples but no practice exercises. Don't worry, you will get plenty of chance to practice in the rest of the book. For a more detailed explanation of Jacoby 2NT, and as a source of many other helpful conventions, you should refer to *25 Bridge Conventions You Should Know*, by Barbara Seagram and Marc Smith. Because Jacoby 2NT is very often the start of a slam bidding auction, two other conventions are frequently used in our practice hands: cuebidding and Blackwood. It is critical that you understand cuebidding, so we've included an explanation of cuebidding here as well. You will also need to ask partner about Aces and Kings, from time to time. In our sample auctions, for demonstration purposes, we will use Roman Keycard Blackwood (1430 version) which is described in another book in this series. However, when you bid the hands just use your own favorite form of Blackwood, regular or Roman Keycard.

The final section of the book, 'Practice Hands', contains a set of forty pairs of North and South hands. You can cut them out or copy them and use them with a partner to practice bidding (don't try to do more than about ten at one sitting — that's more than enough to think and talk about at one time). We have provided space beside each hand to write down your auction; we suggest that you do this so you can refer to it when you are looking at the answers. You can also do this solo if you like: look at each hand in turn and write down the bid you would make at each step of the auction. Getting to the right spot is not the only goal; bidding the hand in the best way is another goal so, even if you see both hands, you will still need to work out the correct auction. When you have finished bidding the hands look at the sample auctions and final contracts suggested in Section 5. There may be more than one way to bid the hand, so don't worry if you don't duplicate our sequence exactly. Focus in particular on your use of Jacoby 2NT and make sure that you got that right.

There is an earlier section of the book, entitled 'Working Alone' which contains the same practice deals. In this section, we show you just one of the hands and ask you a series of questions about how to bid it as the auction develops. Working through these exercises will teach you a lot more about the convention, so even if you go through the practice deals with a partner, we suggest you go through the questions and try to answer them. This will help you to make sure that you understand the convention thoroughly.

A final warning: don't expect to be perfect. Some of these hands are hard. So if you are doing better at the end of the book then at the beginning, you are doing very well indeed.

HOW JACOBY 2NT WORKS

The 2NT Bid and Responses

Opener	**Responder**
1♠ or 1♡	2NT

Jacoby 2NT is a conventional bid used to make a game-forcing raise of a major-suit opening bid. The purpose of this bid is to allow the partnership to commit to game in the major and to probe for a possible slam contract. Since the partnership has at least a nine-card major-suit fit and at least 26 points between the two hands you know you want to be in game. If you have 33 or more points between you, the partnership will usually want to get to slam. However sometimes you have the right magic between the two hands to make a slam even with fewer than 33 points, because of distributional values. You have singletons or voids in all the right places. Jacoby 2NT can help you in your quest to find out if this magic is there.

Look at the example auction above. Opener's first bid was one of a major. Responder responds 2NT (Jacoby) directly if his hand meets the following requirements:

a) at least four-card trump support for partner's major;
b) at least 13 dummy points in support of the major.

This bid is unlimited in strength and responder can have a very good hand.

Here are examples of hands suitable for a Jacoby 2NT response to an opening bid of 1♡:

a) ♠ A 2
    ♡ 10 9 8 7 4
    ◇ A Q 3 2
    ♣ K 2

b) ♠ 9 2
    ♡ A 9 8 7
    ◇ A K Q 3
    ♣ K Q 9

c) ♠ A Q 10 9 8
    ♡ K Q 9 8
    ◇ A 2
    ♣ K 9

d) ♠ K Q J 9 8
    ♡ K 4 3 2
    ◇ A K Q 2
    ♣ —

By contrast, here are examples of hands which are not suitable for
Jacoby 2NT response to 1♡:

a) ♠ 9 3 2
    ♡ 10 9 8 7
    ◇ A Q 3 2
    ♣ K 2

b) ♠ 9 2
    ♡ A K 8
    ◇ A K Q 3
    ♣ K 9 8 2

c) ♠ 9
    ♡ A 9 8 7 4 3 2
    ◇ 3
    ♣ Q 9 8 7

Hand a) is too weak for Jacoby 2NT. This hand is only worth a limit
    raise in hearts not a game force. Invite to game by bidding 3♡.
Hand b) only has three trumps; using Jacoby 2NT promises four
    trumps. Bid 2♣ for now and support hearts later.
Hand c) has a lot of offense but does not have enough points to qual-
    ify for Jacoby 2NT. Just bid 4♡ immediately.

After responder bids Jacoby 2NT, opener now shows responder
more about his hand.

   If opener has an unbalanced hand* he responds as follows:

• Responder bids his singleton or void at the three-level
• With a good quality second suit (at least five cards in length)
  he bids this suit at the four level. Obviously with another five-
  card suit, opener also has a singleton or void but it is more
  important to show partner the second suit.

---

* We're going to use the terms 'balanced' and 'unbalanced' here slightly differ-
ently from the way they are used when describing notrump-type hands. Here,
an 'unbalanced' hand is one with at least one singleton or void, while all other
hands will be described as 'balanced'.

Here are some examples.

Opener	Responder
1♠	2NT

♠ A K 9 8 7
♡ 9
◇ A K Q 3
♣ K 9 8

Opener rebids 3♡ to show the singleton heart.

Opener	Responder
1♠	2NT

♠ K Q 7 3 2
♡ —
◇ A K Q 9 3
♣ Q 9 8

With this hand, opener rebids 4◇ to show the strong five-card diamond suit. Opener should not bid 3♡, his void, since he should give
priority to showing the second suit. (You will see later why this second suit is so important and useful.)

If opener has a balanced hand (no singletons or voids) he selects the
most descriptive of the following:

a) With a minimum hand, he bids four of the major to sign off
b) With 16 total points or more and good trumps, he bids 3 of the
   major
c) With 16 total points or more and poor trumps, he bids 3NT

Here are some examples:

Opener	Responder
1♠	2NT

♠ A K J 8 3 2
♡ 9 2
◇ K 4 3
♣ 9 8

With this hand, opener bids 4♠. This hand is a minimum.

Opener	Responder
1♠	2NT

♠ A K 10 9 8 7
♡ 9 2
◇ A K 3
♣ Q 8

Bid 3♠ this time. This hand meets the requirement of at least 16 total points and good trumps.

Opener	Responder
1♠	2NT

♠ Q 9 8 7 2
♡ A 9
◇ A K 4 3
♣ K 8

This is the hand for a 3NT rebid. Despite having more than 16 total points, it has poor trumps.

The following table summarizes the Jacoby 2NT convention and opener's rebids:

Opener	Responder
1♡	2NT

Opener's rebids:

3♣, 3◇, 3♠	singleton or void in suit bid
4♣, 4◇	good five-card suit
3♡	balanced, 16+, good trumps
3NT	balanced, 16+, poor trumps
4♡	balanced, minimum opener

Opener	Responder
1♠	2NT

Opener's rebids:

3♣, 3◇, 3♡	singleton or void in suit bid
4♣, 4◇, 4♡	good five-card suit
3♠	balanced, 16+, good trumps
3NT	balanced, 16+, poor trumps
4♠	balanced, minimum opener

How the Auction Continues

Hand Re-evaluation

If opener shows an unbalanced hand, then responder (the Jacoby 2NT bidder) needs to re-evaluate his hand in light of his partner's bid. His hand may have improved or worsened. Responder's hand improves when he does not have many high cards opposite opener's shortness. For example, if partner shows shortness in diamonds and responder holds four little diamonds, his hand has improved since there are no wasted diamond points in his hand. All his cards are working. However, kings, queens and jacks in short suits are wasted since partner can ruff this suit and would have preferred these honors to be located elsewhere. For example:

Partner	You
◊ 3	◊ K J 5

Suppose partner shows diamond shortness and you have the ◊ K-J-5. These cards will produce one trick at most (if you can take a winning diamond finesse). If partner has a diamond void you will take no diamond tricks; you may as well have had the ◊ 4-3-2. This is what we mean by wasted values. However it would be great if you happened to have

Partner	You
◊ 3	◊ 5 4 2

or

Partner	You
◊ 3	◊ A 4 2

Here is an example of a hand that improves when partner shows shortness in diamonds:

Partner	You
1♠	2NT
3◊	
♠ A Q 5 4 2	♠ K J 7 6
♡ A 10 7	♡ K Q 4 2
◊ 2	◊ 9 6 5
♣ K 9 5 2	♣ A 4

Partner has little more than a minimum opener but 6♠ has excellent chances. If partner had shown shortness in hearts, your hand would have worsened — you would have wasted honors opposite partner's shortness. If we switch partner's diamonds and hearts, the spade slam becomes a very poor contract:

Partner	You
1♠	2NT
3♦	

♠ A Q 5 4 2	♠ K J 7 6
♡ 2	♡ K Q 4 2
♦ A 10 7	♦ 9 6 5
♣ K 9 5 2	♣ A 4

Holding fitting cards in opener's second suit is also a good thing. For example:

Partner	You
1♠	2NT
4♦	

♠ Q 9 8 7 6	♠ A K 4 3 2
♡ 4	♡ 9 7
♦ A J 10 3 2	♦ K Q 8
♣ A J	♣ 10 8 6

Your hand is a minimum for a Jacoby 2NT raise. However, when partner bids 4♦, showing a strong five-card diamond suit, your hand has improved substantially since your diamond and spade honors are very helpful cards. We've given partner a pretty poor hand, and yet slam is a virtual certainty. But notice that if you swap partner's diamonds with either his clubs or his hearts, there is no slam. In fact, when you combine your hand with any hand that opener is likely to have in this auction you will have good slam chances as long as you do not have two quick losers. You can test this yourself by creating hands for opener that fit the auction (i.e. where he is 5-5 in spades and diamonds).

In summary, *you want to have your high cards opposite partner's length and not opposite his shortness.* This increases the value of your high cards.

Deciding Whether To Try For Slam

If responder's hand has improved then he should make some move to slam even if he has limited extra values. For example,

Opener	Responder
1♠	2NT

♠ A Q 9 8
♡ A Q J 2
◇ 7 6 4
♣ 3 2

with this hand responder should make a slam try if opener rebids 3◇ (diamond shortness) or 4♡ (second suit in hearts) even though he has a minimum for his 2NT bid.

With limited extra values and no good fit, responder should sign off by jumping to game if his hand does not fit well with opener. What do we mean by 'sign off'? When you jump to game it is a signal to partner that from your hand you do not believe that slam will make. If partner has a surprise, something that he has not told you about yet, he can still continue on. On the above hand, then, responder would sign off in 4♠ over opener's 3♣ or 3♡ rebid. With a very strong hand responder may move towards slam even without a good fit. For example,

Opener	Responder
1♠	2NT
3◇	

♠ K J 10 4 3
♡ A Q 3
◇ K Q 4
♣ K 2

Responder has wasted diamond cards, when opener rebids 3◇ over Jacoby 2NT. But responder still has enough values to make a move towards slam. For example, opener might have

♠ A 10 5 4 2
♡ K 10 8 3
◇ 9
♣ A J 7

when slam is an excellent prospect.

What To Do When Opener Has A Balanced Hand

1) Opener has a minimum (rebids four of his major)
If opener shows a balanced hand with no extra values by jump-

ing to game, responder should respect this signoff unless he has considerable extra values of his own. For example, here responder has a balanced hand with 14 HCP:

Opener	Responder
1♠	2NT
4♠	?

♠ Q 9 8 4
♡ K 2
◇ A Q 4 3
♣ K 4 2

What should responder bid now?

Responder should pass since opener has shown a balanced minimum. Opener might have:

♠ A K J 4 3
♡ Q J 9
◇ 10 7 2
♣ Q 3

You certainly wouldn't want to be any higher than 4♠ on this hand. Responder should only bid on with either strong distribution and playing strength or a powerhouse hand, a minimum of 17 total points. In these circumstances, responder may be able to bid Blackwood or invite to slam by bidding beyond game.

Here is a hand which has a lot of playing strength:

♠ Q 10 9 8
♡ A 2
◇ A K Q 9 8 3
♣ 9

This hand has only 15 HCP, but with a strong six-card side suit it has a lot of playing strength opposite a partner with an opening spade bid, and is worth 19 total points. You will make slam any time opener has good spades and even on some other hands as well. Try this hand opposite opener's balanced minimum we showed above:

Opener	Responder
1♠	2NT
4♠	?

♠ A K J 4 3	♠ Q 10 9 8
♡ Q J 9	♡ A 2
◇ 10 7 2	◇ A K Q 9 8 3
♣ Q 3	♣ 9

Here is an example of a balanced hand strong enough to try for slam opposite a signoff:

Opener	Responder
1♠	2NT
4♠	?

♠ K 10 9 8 3 2	♠ A J 5 4
♡ 10 4	♡ A Q 3
◇ A 3	◇ K J 4 2
♣ K 5 3	♣ A 2

With a hand worth 20 support points responder should continue on, and in this case he will reach an excellent 6♠ contract.

2) **Opener has extra values and good trumps (rebids three of his major)**

If opener shows good trumps by bidding three of the agreed major, responder should cuebid whenever he has a decent hand with at least 14 total points (see below for more on cuebids). A signoff should be reserved for a complete minimum since opener has already shown extra values. Responder should cuebid to show a control in case opener has a very good hand and is concerned about control in a specific suit.

Opener	Responder
1♡	2NT
3♡	?

How should responder proceed with each of the following hands?

a)
♠ A 9 3 2
♡ K Q 9 8
◇ 3
♣ K J 3 2

b)
♠ K Q 9
♡ Q J 6 2
◇ J 2
♣ K J 5 2

c)
♠ K 8 7
♡ A 5 4 3
◇ A Q J 3 2
♣ 2

Hand a) Bid 3♠. You have 16 total points so you should show your first-round spade control. You will not make another slam move. The rest is up to partner.

Hand b) Bid 4♡. This is a complete minimum. If partner can make slam opposite this hand, he will bid it himself.

Hand c) Bid 4◇. This is a decent hand with 14+ total points.

3) **Opener has extra values but poor trumps (rebids 3NT)**
When opener rebids 3NT he shows extra values and poor trumps. Responder should sign off by bidding game in the agreed major unless his trumps are of very high quality:

Opener	Responder
1♡	2NT
3NT	?

♠ K J 4 2	♠ A Q
♡ Q 5 4 3 2	♡ J 9 8 7
◇ K 2	◇ A Q 3 2
♣ A K	♣ Q J 3

Responder should sign off in 4♡ here. Although both opener and responder have extra values, slam is not possible because neither of them has good trumps.

On the other hand if responder has good trumps and a better than minimum hand he should make a slam try. Any slam try shows partner good trumps since otherwise responder would sign off. For example, in this auction

Opener	Responder
1♡	2NT
3NT	?

♠ A Q 5 2	♠ K 9 5
♡ J 10 9 5 4	♡ A Q 8 7
◇ K 9	◇ A Q 3 2
♣ A 9	♣ 5 4

responder should not sign off in four of the major since he can help partner out in the trump suit. With 15 total points responder should make a slam try: he should cuebid 4◇, to indicate to opener that slam is possible. In fact, on these two hands, 6♡ is an excellent contract.

Responder Makes A Slam Try

Responder may make a slam move by bidding anything other than game in the agreed trump suit. Here are some ways responder can try for slam:

a) *Bid three of the agreed major* — this shows slam interest and asks partner to cooperate if he has slam interest. For example: you have

Partner	You
	♠ A J 9 5
	♡ 9 8 4
	◇ K Q 3
	♣ K J 3
1♠	2NT
3♡	?

Bid 3♠: this shows slam interest. Note that if you had bid 4♠, it would show no interest in slam. It would also indicate that partner's 3♡ bid had 'turned you off'. In fact, your hand has improved because you have no wasted values opposite opener's 3♡ bid.

b) *Just use Blackwood.* This bid should be reserved for hands where you are sure that you want to be in slam if partner has the required number of controls. You also have to be confident that you are not in danger at the five-level if partner is lacking in controls. Here is an example of a hand where you may wish to bid Blackwood:

Partner	You
	♠ 9 8 7
	♡ K Q 10 3
	◇ A K Q 10 4
	♣ A
1♡	2NT
3♠	?

Partner's 3♠ rebid shows shortness in spades. If partner has an ace, you would like to be in slam. You know now that there is no danger of losing two spade tricks since partner only has at most one card in the spade suit. In fact, if partner has two aces (or one ace and a spade void) your grand slam chances are excellent. Blackwood may be the easiest way to decide where to play the hand. Notice that you are safe at the five-level even in the unlikely case that partner has no aces.

When You Should Not *Use Blackwood.*

- You should not use Blackwood when you have a void. Blackwood will only tell you how many aces partner has, not which aces he has. This is not likely to be useful information.
- When you have two or three small cards in a suit, you should not use Blackwood, as you may lose two tricks very quickly in this suit even if you are only missing one ace.

In both these situations you should use **cuebids** instead. In a Jacoby 2NT auction, after opener's first rebid, any bid of a new suit is by agreement a cuebid. Since you have already agreed on a trump suit, the new suit is never a suggestion to play there instead. It shows a control in the bid suit. A first-round control means that you can win the trick the first time that suit is played: you would need either the ace or a void. A second-round control means that you will normally win the trick the second time the suit is played. You need either the king or a singleton. The first time you bid a new suit, you are showing a first-round control. For example, in this auction:

Partner	You
1♡	2NT
3♡	?

♠ A K 5 4 3
♡ K J 9 3
◇ 5 4
♣ A 2

bid 3♠ showing that you have first-round control of spades. Partner has shown some extra values and good trumps. You are going to be quite pleased if your partner can bid 4◇ showing a diamond control. You do also have the ♣A (first-round control of clubs) But it takes less bidding space to show the spade control (3♠) than to show the club control (4♣) so you cuebid that one first.

See the following pages for more about cuebids.

A Review of Cuebids

As mentioned earlier, a cuebid is a bid made to show a first- or second-round control in any suit but the trump suit. Having a 'control' means that you can stop the opponents from taking too many winners in that suit by winning the trick. Here are examples of controls in the spade suit (hearts are trumps, say):

a) ♠ A 3 2
b) ♠ —
c) ♠ K 5
d) ♠ 6

Cases (a) and (b) are examples of a first-round spade control. If spades are led you will be able to take the first trick. With (a) you will win the ace and with (b) you will trump the spade. Examples (c) and (d) show a second-round control in spades. If the opponents lead spades you will be able to take the second trick. Note that there is some risk in (c) if the spade is led through the ♠K (assuming partner does not have the ♠Q.) However, this still counts as a second-round control.

In order to make a slam your side must have controls in all of the side suits; to make a grand slam, they'll need to be first-round controls. Here is an example of a hand where you can't make slam even though you have many tricks available:

Partner	You
♠ K Q 10 9 7	♠ A J 5 4 3
♡ 9 2	♡ 5 4
◇ A	◇ K Q J 10 9
♣ K Q J 10 9	♣ A

This hand has 15 top tricks. Unfortunately the opponents have the first two heart tricks so even a small slam cannot be made! Your side does not have a heart control.

How do you know if a bid of a new suit is a cuebid? This is easy after one of you has used Jacoby 2NT. Your side has agreed on the trump suit. This means that after opener's rebid over 2NT, a bid in a new suit by responder and any further new suit bid by opener is always a cuebid. Since the purpose of using Jacoby 2NT is to agree on the trump suit and probe for slam, cuebids are a very important follow-up to a Jacoby response.

What suit should you cuebid? You start by bidding first-round controls, bidding your cheapest first-round control first. 'Cheapest' means that you bid the next one up the line in the auction. The advantage of this is that when you bypass one side suit (a side suit is a non-trump suit) you deny having the first-round control in that suit. You then later bid your second-round controls as cheaply as possible.

The auction starts as follows:

Partner	You
1♡	2NT
3♡	?

Think about what you would do next on each of these hands:

a) ♠ 5 4 3 2   b) ♠ 5 4 3 2
   ♡ A Q 3 2   ♡ A Q 3 2
   ◇ K Q J   ◇ A 2
   ♣ A 2   ♣ K Q J

c) ♠ A 3 2
   ♡ A Q 3 2
   ◇ 5 4 2
   ♣ K Q J

With hand (a) bid 4♣. (In this auction spades is the 'cheapest' cue-bid, clubs second and diamonds last.) This shows a first-round club control and denies a first-round spade control. With hand (b) bid 4◇. This shows a first-round diamond control and denies a first-round control in spades or clubs. With hand (c) bid 3♠. This shows a first-round spade control

How Does The Auction Continue After A Cuebid?

If responder cuebids then opener uses the information provided to assess the chances of slam. Often the lack of a cuebid is as helpful as a cuebid. For example, in hand (b) above, partner knows that you do not have a first-round control in either spades or clubs. If partner is missing both of these controls too, then slam is impossible. Or perhaps partner has the black-suit controls, and now knows that slam is likely; he will bid on accordingly. He may just bid the slam, use Blackwood to ask you for aces, or continue to cuebid to get more information from you. If he cuebids, he follows the same pattern as you: first-round controls first, up the line.

In this next example, opener can bid Blackwood.

Opener	Responder
♠ 5 4	
♡ K Q J 10 5	
◇ A K Q 4	
♣ A 2	
1♡	2NT
3♡	3♠ [1]
?	

1. Cuebid

The cuebid really helped. Without the cuebid opener would have been afraid to bid Blackwood because even if their side were only missing one ace (or one keycard, playing that version of Blackwood) they could have two quick spade losers. With spades under control, the five-level is safe and the only question remaining is the number of aces.

In the following example, it is still unclear whether slam will be a good bet. Responder will need a club control and some extra values. Opener explores by cuebidding:

Opener	Responder
♠ K Q	
♡ A 10 7 4 2	
◇ A 5	
♣ Q J 10 3	
1♡	2NT
3♡	3♠ [1]
?	

1. Cuebid

Opener bids 4◇ to show the first-round diamond control and deny a first-round club control. If responder signs off in 4♡, opener will pass. Notice that Blackwood is not very useful on this hand since if partner shows two keycards (or one ace), opener still does not know whether to proceed since he could be missing the ace and king of clubs.

Finally let us look at an auction which involves several cuebids.

Opener	Responder
♠ Q J 10 5 4	♠ A K 9 8
♡ A K J 3	♡ Q 7 2
◇ Q 4 3	◇ A 9 6
♣ 2	♣ A J 2
1♠	2NT
3♣¹	3◇²
3♡²	4♣²
4♡²	6♠²

1. Shortness
2. Cuebid

When opener shows shortness in clubs, responder has a terrific hand but is worried about hearts. Responder cuebids his ◇A. Opener now cuebids the ♡A. Responder is pretty sure that there is slam now but he cuebids his ♣A to see if opener has more to say. He does not show his ♠A since you cannot cuebid a control in the trump suit. Opener does not have a second-round diamond control so he cuebids his second round heart control. This is good news and bad news. There is no heart loser but there is certainly a second-round diamond loser. Opener cannot have a five-card heart suit (since if had one, he would have responded 4♡ to Jacoby, not 3♣) so there will be at most one diamond discard on the hearts, and it seems that there is an inevitable diamond loser. The grand slam is not possible, and responder bids a final 6♠.

This may seem very complicated but even using occasional cuebids combined with Blackwood will make your slam bidding more accurate. For more information and examples on Blackwood, Roman Keycard Blackwood and Cuebidding see *25 Bridge Conventions You Should Know*.

section 3

WORKING ALONE (QUESTIONS)

Deal 1

♠ J 9 8 7
♡ A K 9 5 4
◇ A Q
♣ 9 7

1. If partner opens 1♡ what do you respond? What if he opens 1♠?
2. Over partner's 1♡ bid you respond with Jacoby 2NT:
   a) What do you do if your partner now bids 3◇?
   b) What if he bids 3♣?
   c) What if he bids 3NT?

Deal 2

♠ A Q 7
♡ K J 7 6 2
◇ K 4 3
♣ K J

1. Partner opens 1♠. What should you bid?
2. Partner opens 1♡ and you bid Jacoby 2NT. What should you do over partner's 3♡ rebid?

Deal 3

♠ A K 10 3 2
♡ K J 10 9 2
◇ 3
♣ J 2

1. You open 1♠ and partner bids 2NT. What is your rebid?
2. After bidding Jacoby 2NT and hearing your response, your partner cuebids in clubs. Should you bid on or sign off?
3. What if partner cuebids in diamonds after you respond to his Jacoby 2NT?

Deal 4

♠ A J 9
♡ K Q J 10 9 2
◇ 5 3
♣ A Q

1. Partner bids Jacoby 2NT over your opening 1♡ bid. What is your rebid?
2. Over your response to Jacoby 2NT, partner bids 4♡. What do you do now?
3. If you cuebid 4♠ or 5♣ over 4♡, and partner bids 5♡, should you continue to slam?

Deal 5

♠ K Q J
♡ A K J 9 8 7 6
◇ 9
♣ K 9

1. Partner bids Jacoby 2NT over your opening 1♡ bid. What is your rebid?
2. If your partner shows two aces during the auction, should you bid slam?
3. What would you do if your partner showed three aces?
4. Partner bids 3♡ (limit raise) over your 1♡ bid. Should you try for slam?

Deal 6

♠ A Q 4 2
♡ 8 7
◇ K Q J 9 8
♣ 7 6

1. Partner has opened the bidding 1♠. What is your response?
2. If you used Jacoby 2NT, how would you reply to the following rebids by partner?
   a) Partner rebids 4♠
   b) Partner rebids 3◇
   c) Partner rebids 3♡

Deal 7

♠ K 8 7 6 3
♡ 2
◇ K 6 4 3
♣ 7 6 2

1. Partner opens the bidding with 1♠. Which of the following bids is the correct response and why?
   a) Jacoby 2NT
   b) 2♠
   c) 3♠ (limit raise)
   d) 4♠

Deal 8

♠ K Q 10 8 7
♡ A K Q
◇ 7 6 4
♣ J 8

1. Partner opens the bidding with 1♡. What do you bid?
2. If partner opens 1♠ and you bid Jacoby 2NT, how do you continue after the following rebids:
   a) Partner bids 3◇
   b) Partner bids 3♠
   c) Partner bids 3♡

Deal 9

♠ A J
♡ A K J 9 3 2
◇ 4
♣ A J 10 8

1. What is your opening bid on this hand?
2. If partner responds Jacoby 2NT to your opening 1♡ bid, what should you rebid?
3. What do you think the likely contract is once partner bids Jacoby 2NT?
4. If partner signs off in 4♡ over your rebid, what should you do?

Deal 10

♠ Q J 7 5
♡ A 6 4
◇ 4
♣ K Q J 10 8

1. Partner has opened 1 ♠. What should you bid?
2. You respond with Jacoby 2NT to your partner's 1♠ opening. What should you bid after partner rebids 3♡?
3. What if partner bids 3♣?

Deal 11

♠ A 3
♡ K 10 9 8
◇ A 9 7
♣ Q 6 5 4

1. Partner has opened 1♡ and you bid Jacoby 2NT. What do you do over each of the following rebids from partner?
   a) 3♣
   b) 3♡
   c) 3NT
   d) 4♡
2. The auction has proceeded:

Partner	You
1♡	2NT (Jacoby)
3◇	3♠
4◇	

   What does partner's 4◇ bid mean and what should you do now?

Deal 12

♠ J 10 6 5 3
♡ A Q 7
◇ K Q 9
♣ A Q

1. What should you do on this excellent hand after partner opens 1♠?
2. If you bid Jacoby 2NT and partner rebids 4♠, how would you continue?
3. What would you do if partner rebid 3NT over your Jacoby 2NT?

Deal 13

♠ 9 8
♡ A 10 8 6 5
◇ A 10 4 3
♣ K 4

1. Would you open this hand as dealer?
2. If you open 1♡ and your partner bids 2NT (Jacoby), how do you evaluate your hand now and what would you rebid?
3. If your partner made a limit raise in hearts (1♡-3♡), what would you do?

Deal 14

♠ Q 10 5 4
♡ K 8 3
◇ Q 6
♣ K J 8 3

1. If your partner opens the bidding with 1♠, what should you bid?
2. What would you do if your hand were
   ♠ K 10 5 4   ♡ K 8 3   ◇Q 6   ♣ K J 8 3?
3. What about
   ♠ K 10 5 4   ♡ K 8 3   ◇ K 6   ♣ K J 3 2?

Deal 15

♠ J 4
♡ K Q J 5 3
◇ A Q 5 4
♣ K 5

1. You open 1♡ and partner bids Jacoby 2NT. What is your response? Is there another option?
2. If you rebid 3♡ over Jacoby 2NT, how would you continue if your partner bid the following:
   a) 3♠ ?   b) 4♣ ?   c) 4♡ ?

Deal 16

♠ A Q 10 8 7
♡ K 5
◇ A Q 10 3
♣ 5 2

1. If you open 1♠ and partner makes a limit raise (1♠-3♠), what should you do?
2. You open 1♠ and your partner bids Jacoby 2NT. What is your rebid?
3. If your partner then signs off in 4♠, should you continue?

Deal 17

♠ Q 5 4
♡ A K Q 5 4
♢ 9 8 7 4 3
♣ —

1. You open 1♡ and your partner bids Jacoby 2NT. Which rebid is the best and why?
   a) 4♡
   b) 4♢
   c) 3♣
2. If you rebid 3♣ and your partner cuebids 3♢, what should you do?
3. What would you do if partner bid 3♠ over your 3♣ rebid?

Deal 18

♠ 3
♡ A K 9 8 7 6
♢ A 9 2
♣ A Q 4

1. You open 1♡ and partner responds 2NT (Jacoby). Where do you expect to play this hand?
2. Over your 1♡ bid partner responds 4♣ (a splinter bid, showing 13-15 and short clubs, with four-card heart support). Where do you expect to play the hand?
3. If partner bids 4♣ (splinter) and then signs off in 4♡ over your 4♢ cuebid, what would you do now?

Deal 19

♠ 8 7 6
♡ K 7 6 2
♢ K Q J 3
♣ K 4

1. You bid Jacoby 2NT over partner's 1♡ bid. How would you continue if partner made the following bids.
   a) 3♢ ?
   b) 3♠ ?
   c) 4♡ ?

Deal 20

♠ A K Q 10 7 6 5
♡ A 2
♢ 4
♣ Q 4 3

1. What is the best opening bid on this hand?
2. When partner responds Jacoby 2NT to your 1♠ opening, how do you plan to continue the auction?
3. If you bid 3♢ and partner bids 4♣ what does this tell you?
4. If partner bids 4♢ over 3♢, what does it say about clubs?

Deal 21

♠ A K 8 3 2
♡ A J 10 2
◇ —
♣ K Q J 10

1. You can hardly believe it when partner opens this hand 1♠. Where do you expect to play this hand?

2. Over your Jacoby 2NT response, partner rebids 3♡. What contracts are you considering? What are you trying to find out?

3. What is your plan for the auction, and what is the next bid you will make?

Deal 22

♠ K Q 7 6 3
♡ K 8
◇ A 5
♣ K 9 7 3

1. You have opened this hand 1♠ and your partner has responded 2NT. What is the right rebid — 3♠ or 4♠?

2. If you have rebid 3♠ and partner bids 4♠, should you bid again?

Deal 23

♠ Q 5
♡ Q J 5 2
◇ A 8 4
♣ K J 7 3

1. Partner opens the hand 1♡ and you bid Jacoby 2NT. What would you bid over a 3♠ rebid?

2. If partner rebid 4◇ over your Jacoby 2NT bid, what would you do?

Deal 24

♠ Q J 8 7
♡ A 10 8 7
◇ A J 8
♣ Q 2

1. Partner opens this hand 1♠ and you bid Jacoby 2NT. Here is a list of responses. Indicate which improve you hand, which worsen your hand and which are neutral:
   a) 3◇
   b) 3♡
   c) 3♠
   d) 3NT
   e) 4◇

2. What would you do if partner rebid 4♠ over your 2NT bid?

Deal 25

♠ A K Q
♡ K J 8 6 4
◇ J 8 3
♣ 9 4

1. Partner opens this hand 1♡ and you bid Jacoby 2NT. What is the rebid you would most like to hear from partner?
2. If partner responds 4◇ to your Jacoby 2NT bid, what does it show? Should you sign off in game or keep going?
3. What should you bid next if the auction proceeds as shown below, and why?

Partner	You
1♡	2NT
3♡	3♠
4◇	?

Deal 26

♠ K 9 8 5 3
♡ A 7
◇ K J 10 9 4
♣ 5

1. You open this hand 1♠. What do you reply to partner's Jacoby 2NT and why?
2. If you rebid 4◇ over 2NT, and partner responds 4♡, what does this mean since you have the ♡A?
3. Should you sign off in 4♠ or bid on over partner's 4♡?

Deal 27

♠ 4
♡ A K 5 3
◇ A Q J 10 7 2
♣ 5 4

1. Partner opens the bidding with 1♡. Knowing that you have a heart fit with partner, how many losers do you see in your hand playing in hearts?
2. What cards are you looking for to make slam?
3. What is the advantage of responding Jacoby 2NT?

Deal 28

♠ A 8 7 6 2
♡ A J 9 8
◇ Q 2
♣ K Q

1. You open the bidding with 1♠. What would you rebid if partner bid Jacoby 2NT?
2. After your rebid over Jacoby, partner signs off in 4♠. Should you bid again?

Deal 29

♠ 7
♡ Q J 8 5 2
◇ A 5 4
♣ A 8 7 2

1. You open 1♡ and partner bids Jacoby 2NT. What rebid would you make? Is there a second choice?
2. Over your response partner cuebids 4♣. Does this bid deny the ♠A? What does it show?
3. Would you cuebid 4◇ over 4♣, or not?

Deal 30

♠ 9 8 7 6 3
♡ A K Q 8 5
◇ A
♣ J 2

1. Despite the anaemic-looking spades, you open this hand 1♠. Partner bids 2NT. What is your rebid?
2. Your side heart suit is excellent. If partner signs off in game now, should you bid again?

Deal 31

♠ K 2
♡ J 10 9 8 6 5
◇ A K
♣ K Q 2

1. You open 1♡ and partner bids Jacoby 2NT. What is your correct rebid?
2. If partner bids 4♡ over your rebid; should you bid again? Why? Or why not?

Deal 32

♠ K 7 6
♡ A Q 10 9
◇ A J 8 7
♣ K Q

1. Partner opens 1♡. Where do you think you are going to play this hand?
2. Partner rebids 3◇ over your Jacoby 2NT. Has this made your hand better or worse?
3. What should you bid now?

Deal 33

♠ K 10 9 8 2
♡ K J 9 8
◇ K 2
♣ Q 10

1. You open this hand 1♠ and partner bids Jacoby 2NT. What should you rebid?
2. If you decide to sign off in 4♠, what should you do if partner makes one of the following bids?
   a) 5◇
   b) 5♠

Deal 34

♠ J 10 9 3
♡ J 10 9 4
◇ 2
♣ A K Q 2

1. What bid would you make over partner's 1♡ opening?
2. If partner cuebids spades over your response, should you sign off?

Deal 35

♠ Q 8 3
♡ A 10 9 8 7
◇ A 6 4
♣ A 3

1. You open this hand 1♡. What is your rebid over partner's Jacoby 2NT?
2. Is this hand a maximum for the rebid you chose?
3. If partner makes a move towards slam over your rebid, would you accept his suggestion or not?

Deal 36

♠ A Q J 2
♡ K Q 10 9 8 7
◇ A
♣ Q 2

1. Partner responds Jacoby 2NT to your opening 1♡ bid. What is your correct rebid?
2. What are you hoping that partner will bid next, and why?
3. If partner bids 4♡ at his second turn, will you bid again? If so, what bid will you make?

Deal 37

♠ A K 3 2
♡ A 2
◇ Q 3 2
♣ J 5 4 2

1. Partner opens 1♠ and you bid Jacoby 2NT. How would you continue if partner made one the following rebids:
   a) 3♣ ?
   b) 3♡ ?
   c) 3NT ?
2. Partner rebids 4♡ over your Jacoby 2NT. When you sign off with 4♠ partner persists with 5♣. How do you like your hand now? What should you bid?

Deal 38

♠ K 9 8 5
♡ A 3 2
◇ Q J 3
♣ A 10 2

1. Your partner has opened the bidding with 1♠ and you plan to bid Jacoby 2NT. How do you rate your hand for this action – minimum, intermediate or powerhouse?
2. Has your hand improved if partner rebids 3♣? What about 3◇?
3. Would a rebid of 4◇ from your partner help your hand?
4. What would you do over a 3♡ rebid?

Deal 39

♠ K Q J 5
♡ 9 8 3 2
◇ A Q J
♣ 3 2

1. Is your hand worth more in support of spades or of hearts?
2. If your partner opens with 1♠ and then rebids 4♣ over your 2NT, should you make a move to slam? Why? Or why not?

Deal 40

♠ K Q J 8 5
♡ 3
◇ A 9 8 7
♣ K 4 2

1. You are delighted to hear partner bid Jacoby 2NT over your 1♠ opening. What is your rebid? Would you consider a 4◇ rebid?
2. If your partner bids 4♣ over your rebid, what does that show?
3. What would you bid next over your partner's 4♣?
4. If your partner had bid 4♡ instead of 4♣, what would that tell you about clubs?

WORKING ALONE (answers)

Deal 1

1. Bid Jacoby 2NT in response to an opening bid in either major. You
have strong support for either major suit. For example, in spades
you have 15 dummy points (1 point for the doubleton). Therefore
you have more than enough to bid Jacoby 2NT.
2. a) Sign off in 4♡. Your diamond honors are wasted and your
hand has worsened.
   b) Bid 3◇. Your hand has improved a little bit and is worth a
small move to slam. You will make no further move to slam.
It is now up to your partner.
   c) Bid 4◇. You have more than 14 dummy points. Making a
cuebid indicates that you have some slam aspirations (and
also indicates that your trumps must be good or you would
have no such aspirations after partner has shown poor
trumps). It is important to show partner the quality of your
trumps; now he can make a move if he wishes.

Deal 2

1. Bid 2♡. You have only three spades so you do not meet the
requirements to bid 2NT over 1♠.
2. Bid 3♠. You have a great hand and slam looks likely if partner
has a decent hand with good trumps, as he promises by his 3♡
bid.

Deal 3

1. Bid 4♡. You have a good five-card suit, and you want partner to
value his heart holding. Showing the singleton diamond is not as
important.

2. Bid 6♠, not 5♠. Partner liked your 4♡ bid a lot since he is now bidding past game. Whatever partner is looking for you have it. In fact, you can deduce from the auction that partner is probably looking for a diamond control. If partner had both diamonds and clubs controlled partner would likely have bid Blackwood.

3. Bid 5♠. If partner cuebids 5◇ you have to sign off in 5♠. Your side does not have a first-round club control and the opponents may well have the ♣A and ♣K to cash at the very beginning of the hand.

Deal 4

1. Bid 3♡, showing a good hand with good trumps and extra values.

2. Bid 4♠, a cuebid. Even though partner shows no extra values you still have an excellent chance for slam, but Blackwood won't solve the problem since you do not have a diamond control. You hope that partner will now be able to cuebid diamonds.

3. Pass. Partner is denying a diamond control. Your side has two diamond losers.

Deal 5

1. Bid 4NT -- Blackwood. This hand is solid. If partner has enough aces you are set for slam

2. Bid 6♡. This is a great small slam. It is possible to construct a hand where 6♡ is only 50-50 (needing the ♣A onside) but just barely. This hand will easily make six most of the time.

3. Bid 7NT (or 7♡). You have thirteen tricks and no losers. In fact you can claim 7NT before the opening lead is made!

4. Bid 4NT. This hand is worth a slam try opposite a limit raise. All you really want to know is about aces. If partner has four trumps and two aces, slam will be a very good contract. There is a slight danger that you may go down at the five-level but the risk is low.

Deal 6

1. Bid Jacoby 2NT. This sets the suit, forces to game and emphasizes your spade support.

2. a) Pass. Your hand has no extra values and neither does partner.
   b) 4♠. Oh dear, the whole diamond suit is much less valuable

opposite partner's shortage. This hand has just got a lot worse.

c) Bid 4♠. You don't have enough to move past game when partner shows heart shortness. If you had three hearts and only one club you might have taken a chance.

Deal 7

1. d) 4♠ is the correct bid. 1♠ - 4♠ shows 6-9 HCP and five spades. This is a great bid – both offensively and defensively. With five trumps, a ruffing value and a side king you may even make this and it will certainly be hard for the opponents to find their best contract.

   3♠ shows 10-12 and exaggerates the high card strength of the hand. It will make it hard for the opponents to enter the auction but partner will expect you to have more defense if opponents do bid.

   2♠ does show your spade support and general values but you make it too easy for the opponents to come into the auction

   Using Jacoby 2NT substantially overstates your strength. Partner may push on to slam when there is no realistic chance (or even double an opponent's contract which will make).

Deal 8

1. Bid 1♠. Even though you have very good trumps you promise four of them when you use Jacoby 2NT.

2. a) Bid 3♡ — a cuebid. This hand has become a lot better when partner has shown diamond shortness. You have a good chance of slam now.

   b) Bid 4♡. You have a little bit of extra with the fifth trump and excellent hearts. As partner has extra too, you might make slam. Show partner a heart control.

   c) Bid 4♠. Your hand has become a lot worse. Your great hearts are not especially useful opposite partner's heart shortage.

Deal 9

1. Bid 1♡. The main criterion for deciding whether to open with one of a suit or with 2 ♣ should be, 'Will I miss game if partner passes?' With this hand, even though it is really strong, game is unlikely on any hand partner passes a 1♡ bid unless he has heart

support. If he does have heart support, partner will try very hard to raise.

Suppose partner has ♠932 ♡Q32 ◊653 ♣9432. Partner will pass your 1♡ bid, but 4♡ is a very poor contract. Try to imagine other hands with which partner will pass 1♡, and see what you think. If you open at the one-level there will be more room to bid slowly, and pick the right contract – it may even be in clubs!

2. Bid 3◊, to show the singleton diamond.
3. This hand will be played in slam. The minimum contract you will settle for is 6♡, and 7♡ or 7NT are possible. It will be interesting to see what partner does now over your 3◊ rebid. The extra information can help you decide between six and seven hearts
4. Bid 6♡ or bid 4NT, Blackwood. If partner signed off over 4♡ he likely has wasted diamond cards and a minimum hand. Even if your side has all the aces and kings, that may still only be twelve tricks, so 6♡ is likely to be enough.

Deal 10

1. Bid 2NT. This hand is worth 16 dummy points opposite partner's 1♠ opening bid and you have four trumps so you have the right values for Jacoby 2NT. Even though your club suit is very good your best bid is still Jacoby 2NT. This sets the suit and allows for slam exploration.
2. Bid 4♡. Your hand still looks good after the 3♡ bid since you have no wasted heart points. Show your first-round heart control. Partner will know you do not have first-round control of clubs or diamonds.
3. Bid 4♠. Your clubs are wasted opposite partner's shortness. Your 4♠ bid is a signoff telling partner that you do not have slam interest.

Deal 11

1. a) Bid 4♡. You have the wasted ♣Q opposite partner's club shortage and a hand that is only a minimum. You will leave slam tries to partner.
   b) Bid 3♠. You have 14 dummy points and a hand rich in controls. The rest is up to partner. You will make no further move towards slam if he does not.

c) Bid 4♡. This is a close one. Partner has shown weakness in the trump suit. Your trumps are borderline and you almost certainly have at least one trump loser, maybe two. Even if partner has a very good hand you may need a trump finesse to make the slam.

d) Pass. You do not have enough extra values to try for slam opposite a partner with a minimum hand.

2. Partner has already shown a diamond singleton, so 4◇ must show an even better diamond control. Since you have the ◇A you know that partner has a diamond void. You should sign off in 4♡ now you know that your ◇A is wasted; you do not have enough extra values to continue past game.

Deal 12

1. Bid Jacoby 2NT. This bid will allow you to create a game force and also learn more about partner's hand.

2. Bid 4NT, especially if you are playing Roman Keycard Blackwood. You want to be in slam if you are not missing two keycards (two of the ◇A, ♠A and ♠K). There is very little danger that partner has none of these since there are only eleven other high card points in the deck! With regular Blackwood you will have to decide what to do if partner shows one ace. Keycard Blackwood was designed for hands like this.

3. Bid 4♠. It appears that you are off two2 trump tricks. Opening bidder has poor trumps.

Deal 13

1. Yes. This hand has a good five-card suit, a good rebid, 2½ quick tricks, 11 high card points and some points for distribution. The high cards are well placed with the aces in the long suits.

2. Knowing that partner has four-card trump support has made this hand better. However, this hand is still a minimum. Bid 4♡, a sign off. You don't want partner to push to slam expecting that you have extra.

3. Pass. Even though you have a fit with partner this hand is still not good enough to go to game opposite invitational values from partner.

Deal 14

1. Make a limit raise (i.e. bid 3♠ unless you play Bergen raises). You have only 11 HCP and the doubleton ♦Q is not fully pulling its weight. You have no special distribution. Queens and jacks are worth less than aces and kings. This is not worth Jacoby 2NT, which is forcing to game.

2. Make a limit raise. This hand still has only 12 points and is not worth a game raise.

3. Bid Jacoby 2NT. This one is clear-cut. You now have 14 dummy points and the ♦K6 is definitely better than the ♦Q6.

Deal 15

1. Bid 3♡. Let's look at the choices. You could bid 4♡: this would say that you had a minimum. This hand is too good for that bid with 16 HCP, some distribution and a good quality heart suit. You could consider 4♦ but this should show a good five-card suit. So 3♡ is the best choice: it shows good trumps and some extra values. However, you will not push to slam without help from partner.

2. a) Bid 4♦. This cuebid shows partner your first-round diamond control. It does not promise any new extra values. It just lets partner know that your side does not have two quick diamond losers.

   b) Bid 4♦. Partner has denied a first-round spade control but he may still have a second-round control. Show partner your diamond control.

   c) Pass. If partner has a minimum then you do not have enough extra to push to slam.

Deal 16

1. Bid 4♠. You have enough extra values to bid on to game opposite a limit raise.

2. Bid 3♠. This one is pretty clear-cut. You have a very good 15 HCP with some distribution and an excellent five-card spade suit. So 3♠ describes your hand very well.

3. Pass. You do not have enough extra to try for slam if your partner does not have extra values.

Deal 17

1. Bid 3♣. Your diamond suit is not good enough for 4◊. Even though your hand is a minimum, it is your job to show partner your club shortness.
2. Bid 4♣ (cuebid). Although you have a minimum, partner's diamond cuebid has made your hand better and partner has shown some extra values. Show your partner you have first-round club control. You will make no additional move to slam.
3. Bid 4♡. Partner has denied a first-round diamond control. This has not made your hand any better. You have a minimum hand. It is best to sign off.

Deal 18

1. You expect to play the hand in a heart grand slam unless you are missing an ace.
2. You still expect to play the hand in a heart slam — either a small slam or a grand slam.
3. Bid 4NT, Blackwood, or make another cuebid. It is pretty certain that your side can make 6♡, but you would like to explore for a grand slam.

Deal 19

1. a) Bid 4♡. You hate your hand now. You have a minimum and your lovely diamonds are wasted. Your side is committed to game in hearts so just bid it.
   b) Bid 4♡. Even though partner is showing extra values you have nothing extra. Any slam move will have to be up to partner.
   c) Pass. Both of you have minimums. Slam is not possible

Deal 20

1. Bid 1♠. You might have considered opening 4♠ but this hand is way too good for that bid. You have too many high cards outside spades. Your plan is to open 1♠ and rebid 4♠ over partner's response. This shows a hand with a lot of spades which is too good to open a preemptive 4♠.
2. Partner surprised you by raising spades. Now you want to try for slam. You would like to hear a club cuebid from partner to show

you that you are not off two quick tricks in clubs. Show your diamond singleton now with 3◇, and partner will tell you more about his hand.

3. Partner is showing first-round club control. He is denying first-round heart control but this is not a surprise since you have the ♡A. He is still interested in slam after you showed diamond shortness. Since his spades cannot be very good this suggests that he has high cards in clubs and diamonds. Slam is certain and a grand slam is even possible. You can now bid Blackwood.

4. Partner is showing first-round diamond control. He is therefore denying first-round club control since he is bidding his cheapest first-round control. He is also denying first-round heart control. However, you still have a chance for slam if partner has second round club control. Bid 4♡ now. If partner bids 5♣ he will be showing second-round control in clubs and you can bid 6♠. Your biggest fear is that you are missing the club ace and king.

Deal 21

1. You expect to play this hand in slam. You have a hand worth about 23 dummy points! (A void is worth five points as dummy when you have 4-card support for partner.)

2. You are considering 6♠ or 7♠. Partner has five trumps and a singleton heart. That should be enough to make 6♠ even if partner had no high cards! If partner has the ♣A, seven should have an excellent play. (You would also like partner to have the ♠Q.)

3. Cuebid 4◇, the first-round diamond control, over 3♡ and then keep trying to get partner to cooperate. You are not going to stop until you get to at least 6♠. If partner signs off in 4♠ over 4◇ you will cuebid 5♡, the first-round heart control. Even if partner signs off again by bidding 5 ♠, you will cuebid 6♣, showing the second-round club control.

Deal 22

1. Your correct rebid is 3♠. You have extra values with 17 total points.

2. No. Your hand is not good enough to make another move if partner has a minimum.

Deal 23

1. Bid 4♡. The 3♠ bid has not made your hand any better since the ♠Q is wasted opposite partner's singleton spade. You have a minimum — sign off.

2. You have a diamond fit with partner and the ◇A is a great card. However, your cards in the black suits are not very helpful and you do have a minimum. You cannot afford to bid past game. Sign off in 4♡. If partner bids again you will definitely show your ◇A.

Deal 24

1. a) Improves. You have some length opposite his presumed singleton and only the ◇J is wasted.

   b) Improves. No wastage and length opposite shortness

   c) Neutral. Partner's good trumps mean that slam is still a possibility, though.

   d) Worsens. If partner has poor trumps you are very unlikely to make a slam.

   e) Improves — a lot. Your excellent diamond fit will help partner.

2. Pass. You do not have enough extra values to try for slam opposite partner's minimum.

Deal 25

1. 3◇. Diamond shortness would be great opposite the three diamond losers. (3♣ would be helpful too, but not quite as much.)

2. 4◇ shows a good five-card diamond suit. Bid 4♡ on this hand. While you do have a little extra, the 4◇ bid has not improved your hand. Partner has only three black cards at most so your spade honors are probably wasted. Sign off in game. You would have to bid past game now to make a slam try, and the five-level is too risky. If partner bids on over 4♡, you can show the spade control.

3. Bid 4♡. You have already shown some extra values and the first-round spade control. Your hand is not worth another move.

Deal 26

1. Bid 4◇. This bid shows a good quality five-card diamond suit. If you didn't have all those nice spots the diamonds wouldn't be good enough, but the presence of the ◇10 and ◇9 improve the suit a lot.

2. Partner is showing a first-round heart control. Since you have the ♡A, partner must have a heart void.

3. Bid 4♠. Your ♡A is not pulling its weight opposite your partner's heart void. You have already told partner your story. Time to sign off.

Deal 27

1. You have three or four losers in your own hand. You can assume that you have no heart losers. You have the three black-suit losers and possibly the ◊K.

2. The critical cards on this hand are the ♠A, ♣A, ♣K, ◊K and ♡Q. You don't need all of these but you do need most of them. You need at least second-round club control -- either the ♣A or ♣K. You need at least one black ace so that you do not have two quick black-suit losers. You would like to have the ◊K so that you do not need a finesse in that suit. The ♡Q will also make you feel safer, but with nine hearts you may not have a heart loser anyway.

   This would be an ideal hand for partner: ♠xxx ♡QJxxx ◊Kx ♣AJx. Opposite this hand, slam is cold. A merely good hand from partner would be something like this: ♠KJx ♡Qxxxx ◊xx ♣AQx. If he has this hand, slam will depend on the diamond finesse.

3. You set hearts as trumps and establish a game force. You will be able to find out specific information about partner's hand and start a cuebidding sequence.

Deal 28

1. Rebid 3NT. You have a good hand but your trumps are not good enough for a 3♠ rebid.

2. Pass. We admit that this is borderline. You do have a lot of nice controls and extra values. However partner knows that you have a decent hand and has still signed off. Partner would make an effort to cuebid with even a little bit extra. You probably can't make slam.

Deal 29

1. 3♠. No there is no second choice. You are required to show your singleton whether you like your hand or not.

2. Partner is showing first-round club control. This can only be a void since you have the ♣A. Since clubs is the cheapest first-round control partner may still have the ♠A.

3. No, don't cuebid: sign off in 4♡. You do have a lot of controls and partner has shown slam interest. However, you have the wasted ♣A and a minimum hand.

Deal 30

1. Bid 4♡. This shows partner that you have five good hearts.
2. No. You have already fully shown your hand. You have nothing extra.

Deal 31

1. You should bid 3NT showing a good hand with poor trumps.
2. No. Partner either has a poor hand or he can't help you out in the trump suit. Either way you do not have enough to push for slam. You should pass.

Deal 32

1. Small or grand slam. You have 19 HCP and a fit.
2. Better. You do not have much wasted in diamonds, and you know that you do not need diamond cards from partner to make slam. If partner has the right controls, slam will be guaranteed.
3. Bid 4NT, Blackwood. If partner has both black aces and the ♡K you have enough tricks for a grand slam!

Deal 33

1. Bid 4♠. You have a complete minimum with no singletons or voids.
2. a) Bid 5♠. Partner has enough for slam but is missing a club control. You don't have one either.
   a) Pass. Partner is looking for good trumps. If the only card he needed was the ♠K, partner could have bid Blackwood. Partner might have ♠xxxx ♡A ◇AQJ ♣AKJ98.

Deal 34

1. Bid 4◇, a splinter bid. You have a hand with 13-15 points, four-card trump support and a singleton. A splinter describes this hand perfectly.
2. If partner bids 4♠ (a cuebid) over your 4◇ splinter, you should bid 5♣, showing your first-round club control. You have already

limited your hand when you splinter so you should show partner your control.

Deal 35

1. Bid 4♡. You do not have enough to make a slam try.
2. Yes. You have 14 HCP and one point for the doubleton. This is only one short of the 16 points needed to bid 3♡. This is the most you can have for a sign off.
3. You would cooperate with partner and will not stop short of slam. If partner is interested in slam you must have what partner wants.

Deal 36

1. Bid 3◇. Without a good five-card suit you bid your singleton.
2. You are hoping to hear 4♣. This would indicate a club control, which you need for slam.
3. Yes. Bid 4♠. Although partner has a minimum, your hand needs very little to make slam opposite heart support. If partner has a game raise in hearts you have a good chance for slam. There is very little risk at the five-level. Here is an example of a bad hand for partner: ♠983 ♡AJ43 ◇KQJ2 ♣J9. Even opposite this dummy, you are still safe at the five-level. Try some others and you will see that slam has a good play on any hand where partner has a club control. You cannot bid Blackwood yourself with two quick club losers, so you cuebid your first-round spade control hoping that partner can now cuebid 5♣.

Deal 37

1. a) Bid 3♡. Your hand has improved and is worth a cuebid.
   b) Bid 4♠ Your hand has not improved since you do not have length opposite partner's shortness. You have a minimum, so sign off.
   c) Bid 4♡. Partner has something extra and you have the high trumps partner is missing.
      Your hand has improved a lot. Partner has continued towards slam missing the two high trumps and the heart ace.
2. Bid 5♡. You have a great hand. You could jump right to 6♠, but just in case partner is looking for a grand slam, give him a chance to make another try. You are not stopping short of 6♠.

Deal 38

1. This is a minimum hand. While you do have excellent controls you have no distribution and only 14 HCP.

2. Your hand has improved over 3♣. You have no wasted club cards and no club losers. It worsens over 3◇ since your diamond cards are wasted.

3. You would be very glad to hear a 4◇ response from partner since your diamond cards will help partner. Partner must be short in hearts and clubs and you can stop both those suits. Your hand is so good now you would want to be in slam!

4. Bid 4♣. This bid has improved your hand somewhat. You should cuebid your first-round club control.

Deal 39

1. Initially your hand is better in support of spades since if partner opens 1♡ he may be short in spades and your spade cards will be wasted. If partner has some spade length then your hand will likely play quite well in hearts too.

2. No. You have a minimum hand with no particular club fit. Your diamond cards are not likely to be useful since partner has at least ten cards in the black suits.

Deal 40

1. Bid 3♡. This shows the singleton heart. You need at least five good diamonds to bid 4◇.

2. His 4♣ bid would show first-round club control, likely the ♣A.

3. Bid 4◇. This shows your first-round diamond control. If partner has some extra values now he will bid on and you will be on your way to slam.

4. If partner had cuebid 4♡ instead of 4♣ he would have denied first-round club control. Partner is showing the ♡A.

Deal 1 - Dealer South

NORTH
♠ J 9 8 7
♡ A K 9 5 4
◇ A Q
♣ 9 7

☐

SOUTH
♠ A 6
♡ Q J 8 3 2
◇ K 9 7 3
♣ K Q

NORTH	SOUTH
	1♡
2NT	3NT
4◇	4♡

Deal 2 - Dealer North

NORTH
♠ K 6 5 4 3
♡ A Q 9 8
◇ A J
♣ Q 5

☐

SOUTH
♠ A Q 7
♡ K J 7 6 2
◇ K 4 3
♣ K J

NORTH	SOUTH
1♠	2♡
4♡	4NT
5♠¹	6♡

1. Two keycards with the trump queen.

Deal 3 - Dealer North

NORTH
♠ A K 10 3 2
♡ K J 10 9 2
♦ 3
♣ J 2

☐

SOUTH
♠ Q 9 8 7
♡ A Q 6
♦ Q 9 8 4
♣ A 4

NORTH	SOUTH
1♠	2NT
4♡	5♣
6♠	

Deal 4 - Dealer North

NORTH
♠ A J 9
♡ K Q J 10 9 2
♦ 5 3
♣ A Q

☐

SOUTH
♠ K 8
♡ A 6 5 2
♦ Q 9 8
♣ K J 8 2

NORTH	SOUTH
1♡	2NT
3♡	4♡
4♠	5♡

Deal 5 - Dealer South

NORTH
♠ A 9 8
♡ 10 5 4 2
♦ A 7 4 3
♣ A 2

☐

SOUTH
♠ K Q J
♡ A K J 9 8 7 6
♦ 9
♣ K 9

NORTH	SOUTH
	1♡
2NT	4NT
5♦[1]	7NT

1. Three keycards.

Deal 6 - Dealer North

NORTH
♠ J 9 8 7 6
♡ A K 10 4 2
♢ 7
♣ A 2

☐

SOUTH
♠ A Q 4 2
♡ 8 7
♢ K Q J 9 8
♣ 7 6

NORTH	SOUTH
1♠	2NT
4♡	4♠

Deal 7 - Dealer South

NORTH
♠ K 8 7 6 3
♡ 2
♢ K 6 4 3
♣ 7 6 2

☐

SOUTH
♠ A J 10 7 2
♡ Q 9 8 3
♢ Q 10 8
♣ A

NORTH	SOUTH
	1♠
4♠	

Deal 8 - Dealer South

NORTH
♠ K Q 10 8 7
♡ A K Q
♢ 7 6 4
♣ J 8

☐

SOUTH
♠ A J 6 3 2
♡ 3
♢ K Q 10 9
♣ 7 6 2

NORTH	SOUTH
	1♠
2NT	3♡
4♠	

Deal 9 - Dealer North

NORTH
♠ A J
♡ A K J 9 3 2
◊ 4
♣ A J 10 8

□

SOUTH
♠ Q 3 2
♡ Q 6 5 4
◊ A K 9 8
♣ Q 2

NORTH	SOUTH
1♡	2NT
3◊	4♡
6♡	

Deal 10 - Dealer North

NORTH
♠ A K 9 6 4
♡ 10
◊ K 6 5 3 2
♣ A 9

□

SOUTH
♠ Q J 7 5
♡ A 6 4
◊ 4
♣ K Q J 10 8

NORTH	SOUTH
1♠	2NT
3♡	4♡
4NT	5♣[1]
6♠	

1. One keycard.

Deal 11 - Dealer South

NORTH
♠ A 3
♡ K 10 9 8
◊ A 9 7
♣ Q 6 5 4

□

SOUTH
♠ K Q 9
♡ A J 7 6 5
◊ —
♣ K 9 7 3 2

NORTH	SOUTH
	1♡
2NT	3◊
3♠	4◊
4♡	

Deal 12 - Dealer North

NORTH
♠ Q 9 8 7 4 2
♡ K J
◇ A J
♣ K J 2

☐

SOUTH
♠ J 10 6 5 3
♡ A Q 7
◇ K Q 9
♣ A Q

NORTH	SOUTH
1♠	2NT
3NT	4♠

Deal 13 - Dealer South

NORTH
♠ A K Q 7 6
♡ Q 9 7 3
◇ 7
♣ Q 10 3

☐

SOUTH
♠ 9 8
♡ A 10 8 6 5
◇ A 10 4 3
♣ K 4

NORTH	SOUTH
	1♡
2NT	4♡

Deal 14 - Dealer South

NORTH
♠ Q 10 5 4
♡ K 8 3
◇ Q 6
♣ K J 8 3

☐

SOUTH
♠ A K J 8 7
♡ Q 9 4 3 2
◇ A J 2
♣ 6

NORTH	SOUTH
	1♠
3♠[1]	4♠

1. Limit raise

Deal 15 - Dealer North

NORTH
♠ J 4
♡ K Q J 5 3
◇ A Q 5 4
♣ K 5

SOUTH
♠ A K Q 3 2
♡ A 9 7 6 4
◇ J 2
♣ 8

NORTH	SOUTH
1♡	2NT
3♡	3♠
4◇	4NT
5♠[1]	6♡

1. Two keycards with the trump queen

Deal 16 - Dealer South

NORTH
♠ K 9 5 4 3 2
♡ 10 8 4
◇ K J
♣ A 10

SOUTH
♠ A Q 10 8 7
♡ K 5
◇ A Q 10 3
♣ 5 2

NORTH	SOUTH
	1♠
2NT	3♠
4♠	

Deal 17 - Dealer South

NORTH
♠ K 3
♡ 10 8 7 6
◇ A K
♣ J 7 5 3 2

SOUTH
♠ Q 5 4
♡ A K Q 5 4
◇ 9 8 7 4 3
♣ —

NORTH	SOUTH
	1♡
2NT	3♣
3◇	4♣
4◇	4♡

Deal 18 - Dealer North

NORTH
♠ 3
♡ A K 9 8 7 6
♢ A 9 2
♣ A Q 4

☐

SOUTH
♠ K Q 8 7
♡ Q 10 4 3
♢ K J 6 3
♣ 5

NORTH	SOUTH
1♡	4♣
4♢	4♡
4NT	5♢[1]
6♡	

1. Zero keycards

Deal 19 - Dealer North

NORTH
♠ A K Q 9
♡ Q J 10 4 3
♢ 4 2
♣ 9 8

☐

SOUTH
♠ 8 7 6
♡ K 7 6 2
♢ K Q J 3
♣ K 4

NORTH	SOUTH
1♡	2NT
4♡	

Deal 20 - Dealer South

NORTH
♠ J 9 8 2
♡ Q J 10 5 4
♢ A 2
♣ A 10

☐

SOUTH
♠ A K Q 10 7 6 5
♡ A 2
♢ 4
♣ Q 4 3

NORTH	SOUTH
	1♠
2NT	3♢
4♣	4NT
5♡[1]	5NT
6♣[2]	6♠

1. Two keycards, no trump queen

2. No side kings

Deal 21 - Dealer South

NORTH
♠ A K 8 3 2
♡ A J 10 2
◇ —
♣ K Q J 10

☐

SOUTH
♠ Q J 10 7 6 5
♡ 9
◇ K J 4
♣ A 3 2

NORTH	SOUTH
	1♠
2NT	3♡
4◇	4♠
5♡	6♣
7♠	

Deal 22 - Dealer North

NORTH
♠ K Q 7 6 3
♡ K 8
◇ A 5
♣ K 9 7 3

☐

SOUTH
♠ A 10 5 4
♡ A 5 4
◇ Q 4 3
♣ K 9 7 3

NORTH	SOUTH
1♠	2NT
3♠	4♠

Deal 23 - Dealer North

NORTH
♠ 2
♡ A K 9 6 4
◇ J 10 7 6 3
♣ A 2

☐

SOUTH
♠ Q 5
♡ Q J 5 2
◇ A 8 4
♣ A 2

NORTH	SOUTH
1♡	2NT
3♠	4♡

Deal 24 - Dealer South

NORTH
♠ Q J 8 7
♡ A 10 8 7
◇ A J 8
♣ Q 2

☐

SOUTH
♠ K 10 9 5 4 3
♡ Q J
◇ Q 2
♣ A 7 5

NORTH	SOUTH
	1♠
2NT	4♠

Deal 25 - Dealer South

NORTH
♠ A K Q
♡ K J 8 6 4
◇ J 8 3
♣ 9 4

☐

SOUTH
♠ J 6 2
♡ A Q 7 3 2
◇ A 7 4
♣ K Q

NORTH	SOUTH
	1♡
2NT	3♡
3♠	4◇
4♡	

Deal 26 - Dealer South

NORTH
♠ A Q 7 6 4
♡ K Q 8
◇ Q 7 3
♣ A 3

☐

SOUTH
♠ K 9 8 5 3
♡ A 7
◇ K J 10 9 4
♣ 5

NORTH	SOUTH
	1♠
2NT	4◇
4NT	5♡[1]
6♠	

1. Two keycards, no trump queen

Deal 27 - Dealer North

NORTH
♠ K Q 10 3
♡ Q 9 8 7 6
◇ K 9 8
♣ A

□

SOUTH
♠ 4
♡ A K 5 3
◇ A Q J 10 7 2
♣ 5 4

NORTH	SOUTH
1♡	2NT
3♣	3◇
4♣	6♡

Deal 28 - Dealer South

NORTH
♠ K Q J 10 9 3
♡ 10 4 3
◇ A 9 8
♣ 3

□

SOUTH
♠ A 8 7 6 2
♡ A J 9 8
◇ Q 2
♣ K Q

NORTH	SOUTH
	1♠
4♣	4♠

Deal 29 - Dealer North

NORTH
♠ 7
♡ Q J 8 5 2
◇ A 5 4
♣ A 8 7 2

□

SOUTH
♠ A 10 9 8 5
♡ A 9 6 3
◇ K Q J 6
♣ —

NORTH	SOUTH
1♡	2NT
3♠	4♣
4◇	6♡

Deal 30 - Dealer South

NORTH
♠ A K 10 2
♡ 7 6
◇ K 9 8
♣ Q 9 8 7

☐

SOUTH
♠ 9 8 7 6 3
♡ A K Q 8 5
◇ A
♣ J 2

NORTH	SOUTH
	1♠
2NT	4♡
4♠	

Deal 31 - Dealer North

NORTH
♠ K 2
♡ J 10 9 8 6 5
◇ A K
♣ A J 6

☐

SOUTH
♠ Q 8
♡ K 4 3 2
◇ Q J 9 8
♣ A J 6

NORTH	SOUTH
1♡	2NT
3NT	4♡

Deal 32 - Dealer North

NORTH
♠ A 10 2
♡ K J 6 4 3
◇ 9
♣ A J 3 2

☐

SOUTH
♠ J 7 6
♡ A Q 10 9
◇ A J 8 7
♣ K Q

NORTH	SOUTH
1♡	2NT
3◇	4NT
5◇[1]	5NT
7♡	

1. Three keycards

Deal 33 - Dealer South

NORTH
♠ A Q 4 3
♡ Q 4 3 2
◇ Q J 9
♣ K 2

SOUTH
♠ K 10 9 8 2
♡ K J 9 8
◇ K 2
♣ Q 10

NORTH	SOUTH
	1♠
2NT	4♠

Deal 34 - Dealer North

NORTH
♠ A K Q
♡ A K Q 3 2
◇ 9 8 7 5
♣ 3

SOUTH
♠ J 10 9 3
♡ J 10 9 4
◇ 2
♣ A K Q 2

NORTH	SOUTH
1♡	4◇[1]
4NT	5♣[2]
6♡	

1. Splinter

2. One keycard

Deal 35 - Dealer South

NORTH
♠ A 2
♡ Q J 4 2
◇ Q 5
♣ K J 7 6 2

SOUTH
♠ Q 8 3
♡ A 10 9 8 7
◇ A 6 4
♣ A 3

NORTH	SOUTH
	1♡
2NT	4♡

Deal 36 - Dealer North

NORTH
♠ A Q J 2
♡ K Q 10 9 8 7
♢ A
♣ Q 2

☐

SOUTH
♠ K 6 5
♡ J 6 3 2
♢ K J 9
♣ A J 6

NORTH	SOUTH
1♡	2NT
3♢	4♡
4♠	5♣
6♡	

Deal 37 - Dealer South

NORTH
♠ A K 3 2
♡ A 2
♢ Q 3 2
♣ J 5 4 2

☐

SOUTH
♠ Q J 10 9 8 7
♡ K Q J 10 9
♢ A
♣ A

NORTH	SOUTH
	1♠
2NT	4♡
4♠	5♣
5♡	5NT[1]
7♠	7NT

1. Grand Slam Force (asks for two of the top three trump honors)

Deal 38 - Dealer South

NORTH
♠ K 9 8 5
♡ A 3 2
♢ Q J 3
♣ A 10 2

☐

SOUTH
♠ A 10 4 3 2
♡ K
♢ K 9 8 5
♣ Q J 3

NORTH	SOUTH
	1♠
2NT	3♡
4♣	4♠

Deal 39 - Dealer North

NORTH
♠ 3
♡ A Q J 10 4
♢ 4 2
♣ A Q 10 9 8

☐

SOUTH
♠ K Q J 5
♡ 9 8 3 2
♢ A Q J
♣ 3 2

NORTH	SOUTH
1♡	2NT
4♣	4♡

Deal 40 - Dealer North

NORTH
♠ K Q J 8 5
♡ 3
♢ A 9 8 7
♣ K 4 2

☐

SOUTH
♠ A 10 9 7
♡ 8 5 4 2
♢ K Q 10
♣ A 10

NORTH	SOUTH
1♠	2NT
3♡	4♣
4♢	5♢
6♠	

section
PRACTICE HANDS

Hand 1 - Dealer South

♠ J 9 8 7
♡ A K 9 4 2
◇ A Q
♣ 9 7

YOUR AUCTION

NORTH   SOUTH

Hand 2 - Dealer North

♠ K 6 5 4 3
♡ A Q 9 8
◇ A J
♣ Q 5

YOUR AUCTION

NORTH   SOUTH

Hand 3 - Dealer North

♠ A K 10 3 2
♡ K J 10 9 2
◇ 3
♣ J 2

YOUR AUCTION

NORTH   SOUTH

Hand 4 - Dealer North

♠ A J 9
♡ K Q J 10 9 2
◇ 5 3
♣ A Q

YOUR AUCTION

NORTH   SOUTH

Hand 5 - Dealer South

♠ A 9 8
♡ 10 5 4 2
◇ A 7 4 3
♣ A 2

YOUR AUCTION

NORTH   SOUTH

Hand 6 - Dealer North

♠ J 9 8 7 6
♡ A K 10 4 2
◇ 7
♣ A 2

YOUR AUCTION

NORTH	SOUTH

Hand 7 - Dealer South

♠ K 8 7 6 3
♡ 2
◇ K 6 3 4
♣ 7 6 2

YOUR AUCTION

NORTH	SOUTH

Hand 8 - Dealer South

♠ K Q 10 8 7
♡ A K Q
◇ 7 6 4
♣ J 8

YOUR AUCTION

NORTH	SOUTH

Hand 9 - Dealer North

♠ A J
♡ A K J 9 3 2
◇ 4
♣ A J 10 8

YOUR AUCTION

NORTH	SOUTH

Hand 10 - Dealer North

♠ A K 9 6 4
♡ 10
◇ K 6 5 3 2
♣ A 9

YOUR AUCTION

NORTH	SOUTH

Hand 11 - *Dealer South*

♠ A 3
♡ K 10 9 8
◇ A 9 7
♣ Q 6 5 4

YOUR AUCTION

NORTH	SOUTH

Hand 12 - *Dealer North*

♠ Q 9 8 7 4 2
♡ K J
◇ A J
♣ K J 2

YOUR AUCTION

NORTH	SOUTH

Hand 13 - *Dealer South*

♠ A K Q 7 6
♡ Q 9 7 3
◇ 7
♣ Q 10 3

YOUR AUCTION

NORTH	SOUTH

Hand 14 - *Dealer South*

♠ Q 10 5 4
♡ K 8 3
◇ Q 6
♣ K J 8 3

YOUR AUCTION

NORTH	SOUTH

Hand 15 - *Dealer North*

♠ J 4
♡ K Q J 5 3
◇ A Q 5 4
♣ K 5

YOUR AUCTION

NORTH	SOUTH

Hand 16 - Dealer South

♠ K 9 5 4 3 2
♡ 10 8 4
◇ K J
♣ A 10

YOUR AUCTION

NORTH	SOUTH

Hand 17 - Dealer South

♠ K 3
♡ 10 8 7 6
◇ A K
♣ J 7 5 3 2

YOUR AUCTION

NORTH	SOUTH

Hand 18 - Dealer North

♠ 3
♡ A K 9 8 7 6
◇ A 9 2
♣ A Q 4

YOUR AUCTION

NORTH	SOUTH

Hand 19 - Dealer North

♠ A K Q 9
♡ Q J 10 4 3
◇ 4 2
♣ 9 8

YOUR AUCTION

NORTH	SOUTH

Hand 20 - Dealer South

♠ J 9 8 2
♡ Q J 10 5 4
◇ A 2
♣ A 10

YOUR AUCTION

NORTH	SOUTH

Hand 21 - Dealer South

♠ A K 8 3 2
♡ A J 10 2
◇ —
♣ K Q J 10

YOUR AUCTION

NORTH	SOUTH

Hand 22 - Dealer North

♠ K Q 7 6 3
♡ K 8
◇ A 5
♣ K 9 7 3

YOUR AUCTION

NORTH	SOUTH

Hand 23 - Dealer North

♠ 2
♡ A K 9 6 4
◇ J 10 7 6 3
♣ A 2

YOUR AUCTION

NORTH	SOUTH

Hand 24 - Dealer South

♠ Q J 8 7
♡ A 10 8 7
◇ A J 8
♣ Q 2

YOUR AUCTION

NORTH	SOUTH

Hand 25 - Dealer South

♠ A K Q
♡ K J 8 6 4
◇ J 8 3
♣ 9 4

YOUR AUCTION

NORTH	SOUTH

Hand 26 - Dealer South

♠ A Q 7 6 4
♡ K Q 8
◇ Q 7 3
♣ A 3

YOUR AUCTION	
NORTH	SOUTH

Hand 27 - Dealer North

♠ K Q 10 3
♡ Q 9 8 7 6
◇ K 9 8
♣ A

YOUR AUCTION	
NORTH	SOUTH

Hand 28 - Dealer South

♠ K Q J 10 9 3
♡ 10 4 3
◇ A 9 8
♣ 3

YOUR AUCTION	
NORTH	SOUTH

Hand 29 - Dealer North

♠ 7
♡ Q J 8 5 2
◇ A 5 4
♣ A 8 7 2

YOUR AUCTION	
NORTH	SOUTH

Hand 30 - Dealer South

♠ A K 10 2
♡ 7 6
◇ K 9 8
♣ Q 9 8 7

YOUR AUCTION	
NORTH	SOUTH

Hand 31 - Dealer North

♠ K 2
♡ J 10 9 8 6 5
◇ A K
♣ K Q 2

YOUR AUCTION

NORTH	SOUTH

Hand 32 - Dealer North

♠ A 10 2
♡ K J 6 4 3
◇ 9
♣ A J 3 2

YOUR AUCTION

NORTH	SOUTH

Hand 33 - Dealer South

♠ A Q 4 3
♡ Q 4 2
◇ Q J 9
♣ K 2

YOUR AUCTION

NORTH	SOUTH

Hand 34 - Dealer North

♠ A K Q
♡ A K Q 3 2
◇ 9 8 7 5
♣ 3

YOUR AUCTION

NORTH	SOUTH

Hand 35 - Dealer South

♠ A 2
♡ Q J 4 2
◇ Q 5
♣ K J 7 6 2

YOUR AUCTION

NORTH	SOUTH

Hand 36 - Dealer North

♠ A Q J 2
♡ K Q 10 9 8 7
◇ A
♣ Q 2

YOUR AUCTION

NORTH	SOUTH

Hand 37 - Dealer South

♠ A K 3 2
♡ A 2
◇ Q 3 2
♣ J 5 4 2

YOUR AUCTION

NORTH	SOUTH

Hand 38 - Dealer South

♠ K 9 8 5
♡ A 3 2
◇ Q J 3
♣ A 10 2

YOUR AUCTION

NORTH	SOUTH

Hand 39 - Dealer North

♠ 3
♡ A Q J 10 4
◇ 4 2
♣ A Q 10 9 8

YOUR AUCTION

NORTH	SOUTH

Hand 40 - Dealer North

♠ K Q J 8 5
♡ 3
◇ A 9 8 7
♣ K 4 2

YOUR AUCTION

NORTH	SOUTH

Hand 1 - Dealer South

♠ A 6
♡ Q J 8 3 2
◇ K 9 7 3
♣ K Q

| **YOUR AUCTION** | |
| NORTH | SOUTH |

Hand 2 - Dealer North

♠ A Q 7
♡ K J 7 6 2
◇ K 4 3
♣ K J

| **YOUR AUCTION** | |
| NORTH | SOUTH |

Hand 3 - Dealer North

♠ Q 9 8 7
♡ A Q 6
◇ Q 9 8 4
♣ A 4

| **YOUR AUCTION** | |
| NORTH | SOUTH |

Hand 4 - Dealer North

♠ K 8
♡ A 6 5 2
◇ Q 9 8
♣ K J 8 2

| **YOUR AUCTION** | |
| NORTH | SOUTH |

Hand 5 - Dealer South

♠ K Q J
♡ A K J 9 8 7 6
◇ 9
♣ K 9

| **YOUR AUCTION** | |
| NORTH | SOUTH |

Hand 6 - Dealer North

♠ A Q 4 2
♡ 8 7
◇ K Q J 9 8
♣ 7 6

YOUR AUCTION

NORTH	SOUTH

Hand 7 - Dealer South

♠ A J 10 7 2
♡ Q 9 8 3
◇ Q 10 8
♣ A

YOUR AUCTION

NORTH	SOUTH

Hand 8 - Dealer South

♠ A J 6 3 2
♡ 3
◇ K Q 10 9
♣ 7 6 2

YOUR AUCTION

NORTH	SOUTH

Hand 9 - Dealer North

♠ Q 3 2
♡ Q 6 5 4
◇ A K 9 8
♣ Q 2

YOUR AUCTION

NORTH	SOUTH

Hand 10 - Dealer North

♠ Q J 7 5
♡ A 6 4
◇ 2
♣ K Q J 10 8

YOUR AUCTION

NORTH	SOUTH

Hand 11 - Dealer South

♠ K Q 9
♡ A J 9 7 6
♢ —
♣ K 9 7 3 2

YOUR AUCTION

NORTH   SOUTH

Hand 12 - Dealer North

♠ J 10 6 5 3
♡ A Q 7
♢ K Q 9
♣ A Q

YOUR AUCTION

NORTH   SOUTH

Hand 13 - Dealer South

♠ 9 8
♡ A 10 8 6 5
♢ A 10 4 3
♣ K 4

YOUR AUCTION

NORTH   SOUTH

Hand 14 - Dealer South

♠ A K J 8 7
♡ Q 9 4 3
♢ A J 2
♣ 6

YOUR AUCTION

NORTH   SOUTH

Hand 15 - Dealer North

♠ A K Q 3 2
♡ A 9 7 6 4
♢ J 2
♣ 8

YOUR AUCTION

NORTH   SOUTH

Hand 16 - Dealer South

♠ A Q 10 8 7
♡ K 5
◇ A Q 10 3
♣ 5 2

YOUR AUCTION

NORTH	SOUTH

Hand 17 - Dealer South

♠ Q 5 4
♡ A K Q 5 4
◇ 9 8 7 4 3
♣ —

YOUR AUCTION

NORTH	SOUTH

Hand 18 - Dealer North

♠ K Q 8 7
♡ Q 10 4 3
◇ K J 6 3
♣ 5

YOUR AUCTION

NORTH	SOUTH

Hand 19 - Dealer North

♠ 8 7 6
♡ K 7 6 2
◇ K Q J 3
♣ K 4

YOUR AUCTION

NORTH	SOUTH

Hand 20 - Dealer South

♠ A K Q 10 7 6 5
♡ A 2
◇ 4
♣ Q 4 3

YOUR AUCTION

NORTH	SOUTH

Hand 21 - Dealer South

♠ Q J 10 7 6 5
♡ 9
◇ K J 4
♣ A 3 2

YOUR AUCTION

NORTH	SOUTH

Hand 22 - Dealer North

♠ A 10 5 4
♡ A 5 4
◇ Q 4 3
♣ Q J 2

YOUR AUCTION

NORTH	SOUTH

Hand 23 - Dealer North

♠ Q 5
♡ Q J 5 2
◇ A 8 4
♣ K J 7 3

YOUR AUCTION

NORTH	SOUTH

Hand 24 - Dealer South

♠ K 10 9 5 4 3
♡ Q J
◇ Q 2
♣ A 7 5

YOUR AUCTION

NORTH	SOUTH

Hand 25 - Dealer South

♠ J 6 2
♡ A Q 7 3 2
◇ A 7 4
♣ K Q

YOUR AUCTION

NORTH	SOUTH

Hand 26 - Dealer South

♠ K 9 8 5 3
♡ A 7
♢ K J 10 9 4
♣ 5

YOUR AUCTION	
NORTH	SOUTH

Hand 27 - Dealer North

♠ 4
♡ A K 5 3
♢ A Q J 10 7 2
♣ 5 4

YOUR AUCTION	
NORTH	SOUTH

Hand 28 - Dealer South

♠ A 8 7 6 2
♡ A J 9 8
♢ Q 2
♣ K Q

YOUR AUCTION	
NORTH	SOUTH

Hand 29 - Dealer North

♠ A 10 9 8 5
♡ A 9 6 3
♢ K Q J 6
♣ —

YOUR AUCTION	
NORTH	SOUTH

Hand 30 - Dealer South

♠ 9 8 7 6 3
♡ A K Q 8 5
♢ A
♣ J 2

YOUR AUCTION	
NORTH	SOUTH

Hand 31 - Dealer North

♠ Q 8
♡ K 4 3 2
◇ Q J 9 8
♣ A J 6

YOUR AUCTION

NORTH	SOUTH

Hand 32 - Dealer North

♠ K 7 6
♡ A Q 10 9
◇ A J 8 7
♣ K Q

YOUR AUCTION

NORTH	SOUTH

Hand 33 - Dealer South

♠ K 10 9 8 2
♡ K J 9 8
◇ K 2
♣ Q 10

YOUR AUCTION

NORTH	SOUTH

Hand 34 - Dealer North

♠ J 10 9 3
♡ J 10 9 4
◇ 2
♣ A K Q 2

YOUR AUCTION

NORTH	SOUTH

Hand 35 - Dealer South

♠ Q 8 3
♡ A 10 9 8 7
◇ A 6 4
♣ A 3

YOUR AUCTION

NORTH	SOUTH

Hand 36 - Dealer North

♠ K 5 6
♡ J 6 3 2
◇ K J 9
♣ A J 6

YOUR AUCTION

NORTH	SOUTH

Hand 37 - Dealer South

♠ Q J 10 9 8 7
♡ K Q J 10 9
◇ A
♣ A

YOUR AUCTION

NORTH	SOUTH

Hand 38 - Dealer South

♠ A 10 4 3 2
♡ K
◇ K 9 8 5
♣ Q J 3

YOUR AUCTION

NORTH	SOUTH

Hand 39 - Dealer North

♠ K Q J 5
♡ 9 8 3 2
◇ A Q J
♣ 3 2

YOUR AUCTION

NORTH	SOUTH

Hand 40 - Dealer North

♠ A 10 9 7
♡ 8 5 4 2
◇ K Q 10
♣ A 10

YOUR AUCTION

NORTH	SOUTH